OFFICE POLITICS KNOW THE ENEMY

UNDERSTANDING THE PERSONALITIES AT WORK THAT DRIVE YOU CRAZY

L D FORESTER

All the names in the sections of this book have been changed to protect the guilty.

Printed in the United States of America

First Edition –2018

Paperback
978-0-9911007-8-1
0-9911007-8-6

LD Media and Twin Oaks Publishing
Copyright © 2018

DEDICATION

To my dad, who always
believed in me.

CONTENTS

About the Author

LD Forester achieved an undergraduate degree in Economics and Mathematics at 19 years young, and has worked with small startups to mega firms since the 1980's.

LD was a technology VP for one of the largest global financial institutions in the world, but opted to move to mostly consultancy in the late 1990's.

"I've found more financial gain, freedom and life balance through consultancy. Everyone has something that makes them feel purposeful. Mine is helping others. Consultancy has allowed me more time to do the things that I love like world travel and volunteering."

Having experienced and understanding many different business cultures, interesting personalities, work habits and tactics of people behaving badly has helped LD navigate toxic work environments and foster new ways to help thrive when others failed.

INTRODUCTION

It's funny how things work. I would have never thought about writing this book if a friend hadn't planted that seed in my head. And yet here I am, putting pen to paper, or in this case, putting fingers to keyboard as I share with you ways to survive and even thrive at the workplace.

It's not immediately apparent to the people I meet or those who view my website, that my undergraduate degree focus was in economics and applied mathematics, and that I have a corporate background spanning over 30 years. But yes, it's true, with decades working for corporations, the last full time position as a technology vice president for one of the largest global financial institutions in the world, I certainly have had my fair share of experiences with the stress of deadlines and corporate politics as well as having interacted with some interesting personalities.

I believe that we've all at times felt the sting of the personalities and situations that have left us feeling less than exuberant. You know what I'm talking about here; situations that have tied you in knots, brought you to tears, or caused you fury, envy or disappointment. There is however another way to view and react.

Having worked as both a full-time associate and a consultant in past decades has helped me put things into perspective as I share an accumulated almost 4 decades of experience. Some may make you laugh, some cry, and others get you downright angry as you relate to situations and personalities in these pages.

I've utilized and honed skills to see things in a more holistic way when on corporate assignments that supplement my new way of living, to understand the root cause of the personalities I encounter for a more enjoyable workplace experience.

This book is my way of helping everyone who works for a company, no matter their age, industry, education level or the size of the organization.

My hope is that there's something in these pages that will resonate with you to help you realize that there are more important things in your life to react to than a certain personality or office situation.

Believe me that once you put yourself on the outside of the aquarium, you're better equipped to interact with all its inhabitants.

We're all continually evolving and growing as we do our life homework and our reaction is actually a great indicator of the areas where we need to pause and take time in self-examination.

You'll gain new perspective and insight as you realize that your situation is not unique. Who knows, you may even resolve and release some past hurt or realize that *Johnny* was acting that way because he's going through something himself, as you read these raw and honest accountings.

INTRODUCTION

What I've determine after almost 40 years is that the world does not revolve around me and that people are not interested in going out of their way to hurt me.

We're all dealing with our own life challenges. Most times people are oblivious that how they act has an effect on others. Whether conscious of it or not, when people get our focus to maintain their state of preservation, it's our reaction that impacts us.

OFFICE POLITICS: KNOW THE ENEMY

SECTION 1 – OFFICE POLITICS: PEOPLE BEHAVING BADLY

In this section I describe several topics relative to office politics as well as a plethora of interesting personalities or what I affectionately call, *people behaving badly*.

I'm pointing them all out here, listing these personalities in alphabetical order, these individuals or groups that, if we allow them, can tie us in knots.

I'm sharing a few of my experiences as well as a handful of some of the heard hundreds of stories from the past 3 decades to help you gain insight. Who knows, you may even think after reading this section that you have it good after all.

You will come away with an understanding of the true energy behind these personalities and guidance for better ways to approach and deal with them at the workplace.

How We React
The question you have to ask yourself: *Why am I reacting to this in a nonproductive way?*

I've found that it is usually due to some prior belief or issue that you have "stuck" in your consciousness from a past time that comes to the surface.

How would you like a few steps you can take in order to realize and process this information to effectively eliminate the effect on you?

Identifying and understanding the personalities that you're dealing with allows you to prepare yourself prior to interactions with one of these people, so you're not caught off guard.

Knowing them aids you in adjusting your reactions to these encounters. You'll notice that you don't feel drained, beaten, or upset after the interaction. The smaller a reaction you provide to them, the less likely they will be coming back to you for their fix. Why would they, if they are not going to get the rush they're craving.

Some people are so hung up on rising to the top that they have no regard for the people that are in their way. Some even go out of their way to build themselves up by putting others down by word or deed.

The next section of this book delves into these specific personalities.

THE ARROGANT PRICK

You may have already surmised, these individuals at the office come across to everyone they meet acting somehow superior. They're opinionated, and speak to everyone, including at times, their own management with condescendence. It almost seems as if they don't see any perceived value in anyone else's opinion but their own.

Understandably, it's not pleasant dealing with the arrogant prick, since the way that they behave builds themselves up, at the expense of making others feel small.

I've had many a talk with friends who are so unable to work with these people that they leave their department or even their firm.

Understanding the Arrogant Prick
In the list of all the personalities in this book, the arrogant jerk is probably the most insecure. Knowing that makes me have more empathy for them, as they compensate for their incredible insecurity by acting out in this manner.

The person behind the arrogant jerk personality usually has no idea that's how they come across.

I remember dealing with a man, actually he was more of a boy, in his mid-twenties, still green from college, assigned to work with me when I was leading large technology projects. In meetings, the line of business lead tried not to laugh at his serious demeanor.

He was very smart, but his arrogance turned people off. What he didn't realize is that once you start working in a firm, no one cares what college you graduated from or your grades. I kept thinking, *'Welcome back to kindergarten, kid.'*

With over 20 years of experience in mergers and acquisitions technology project management at that time, even *I* found his attitude offensive.

I had to stop and take a long hard look at myself to determine what it was about this guy that bothered me so much? Then it hit me. He was helping mirror insecurities I had about my own abilities. If I was totally secure, then his poor behavior would not have caused me the slightest concern. It is those individuals that we interact with in life that are our best teachers. Once I realize the role that he was playing, I silently thanked him for bringing to light the areas in my own life where I needed additional work.

Dealing with the Arrogant Prick
If the mere mention of this personality brings back memories and makes you recoil, leaving a bad taste in your mouth or incites anger, then it's hitting that nerve for a reason.

Remember that you are inferior to no one. As a matter a fact it's the arrogant jerk who is feeling inferior to everyone, that's why they act so poorly toward others with an over inflated unjustified ego.

You'll notice that even the most intelligent of these individuals will not be the ones getting promoted, frankly because executive management doesn't like the way that they treat others. Unfortunately they're clueless why others are promoted around them.

In my experience, it's best not to react in any way to this personality. And over complimenting them to gain their friendship is only a waste of time, so is butting heads with them. And pointing out their arrogance may make it worse.

Eventually, if they're smart, they'll realize that their attitude is keeping them back at the office and in life as a whole, and they'll take steps to become more secure.

In life, you often see people who act arrogant. These are usually the people with the shiniest toys, draping themselves over their flashy cars. I think you've all met someone like this outside the office, as I point out this example to help you realize that this is the same person, over compensating for their shortcomings and insecurity by their arrogance.

Take heart my friends and breathe in deeply as you do not react to this personality.   It's not about you!

OFFICE POLITICS: KNOW THE ENEMY

THE AUTHORITY UNDERMINER

Let's talk a minute about individual co-workers, groups or managers who feel the need to undermine your authority. I've seen this happen and also experienced it many times.

An example that comes to mind was when I was a consultant managing large quality groups for a company, joining to assist during a time of great volatility. There were several full time managers in this program, but Doris stood out in the crowd, she went out of her way to undermine the authority of all her peer managers.

Each manager had areas where they were accountable. We would communicate to our respective teams, copying each other for cross functional projects.

Doris would broadcast changes to all team members without sending them first through peer management channels, so we could assess the impact to our projects and sync up. These updates and sometimes different information and deadlines, caused more confusion in an already chaotic environment.

It was a very frustrating time. When I questioned her on it, she threw back at me nonsense babble and double talk in an attempt to cover her tracks.

Was this behavior healthy for anyone else in the program?   No, it wasn't. Not only was it unproductive and confusing to the teams getting mixed messages, it added complete frustration to the peer managers she undermined.

I did not have the authority to force a change in her behavior. I tried to understand what she was doing and ensured that my people were kept well informed.

Understanding the Authority Underminer
I sat in quiet contemplation to see if something would come to light. Finally the answers came. With all the unpredictability and continual changes in the workplace, Doris was petrified. Her attempts to undermine others authority gained her back a little power. After realizing what was going on I invited her to tea where I broached the subject of change with compassion. Tears welled in her eyes as she broke down admitting she was overwhelmed. Her communication from that day forward more forthcoming as she realized she had an ally.

Another example is more recent with an analyst named Manny, who had been working with a team for several years. He was very good at what he did, but lost it when the company assigned Bart as a layer above him to manage each project following PMO standards. Bart was assigned to work with him and by his accounting, Manny was one of the rudest, meanest disrespectful people he had ever worked with, who did everything he could to exclude this new layer above him. I sat there in disbelief as he provided examples of his belligerence, basically calling him out in meetings he was chairing, asking him to justify his participation. I felt sorry for

Manny, who obviously feared change, not embracing it, but opposing it at every turn.

One of the more detrimental examples of authority undermining has to do with management assigning authority to a lower level manager or direct report, only to micro manage what they have assigned and go around this person with whom they entrusted this authority, providing decisions and direction directly to staff. This is the worst sort of undermining of authority, since now staff has no clear point of contact for decisions and guidance. Out of all the experiences in corporate America, this has to be the most destructive to success. Just imagine John getting direction, perhaps different guidance from more than 1 source for any given situation. And who does he listen to? The person who was provided with the authority to lead the project, or the manager above them who did not step back?

In looking at this in-depth, one realizes that this upper manager tried to give up control, yet, just couldn't. This could be for several reasons, but most likely they wanted to feed their ego, believing that nothing can be accomplished without their involvement.

Dealing with the Authority Underminer
The first thing you should do is to take a deep breath and slowly exhale, as you formulate the correct words in response. Knowing that these people are acting this way out of fear may help you have a more compassionate view toward them. You can calmly speak to them and tell them how their behavior is making it difficult for you to perform your job.

If they're not open to acknowledge their poor behavior, like in the cases in the examples I've shared, then you're better trying to limit your interaction with them as much as you can, while still performing your job function.

THE BACKSTABBER

I think we've all experienced someone at the office that has set us up, only to turn around and do something that has felt as if they've lunged a knife into our backs. My full definition of a backstabber is someone who pretends to be your office friend, only to stab you when you're not looking. They may even become close to you as you share lunch together, and perhaps even after work activities. They certainly lead you to believe that they're your close friend, while behind your back they're speaking poorly about your work performance to your co-workers and management. It's not until the truth eventually surfaces that you realize what's been going on.

I remember back when I was working in New York City, when my friend Kathy had applied for a new position that would be deemed a promotion. I could see the excitement in her eyes at the thought of moving over to this area. That excitement grew exponentially when she was told that her application was being considered. She shared the good news with a few of her officemates, one of them named Mandy.

I knew Mandy. I was polite, but also smart enough to steer clear of her. There was just something about her that was a little too ambitious and too quick to judge, when I heard her speaking to others.

When Mandy found out about the position from Kathy, she also decided to throw her hat in the ring, quietly applying for the same job. I'm not saying that there was anything wrong with two co-workers applying for the same position, but it was what Mandy did next that defined her moral compass and set her apart as the backstabber.

During the entire vetting process, Mandy made sure that she and Kathy became the best of friends. She invited her to lunch and probed her, trying to glean any information she could gather and possibly use against her, to show her weaknesses to upper management. I would find out later that she asked Kathy if she and her husband were planning to have a family, what she liked and hated about the company, what she found difficult in her current position and so on.

Mandy then used the information she had gathered, out of context, and spread inflammatory statements around the office about Kathy. It wasn't until one of her co-workers, Susan, went to lunch with Kathy and myself, did the cat finally peak its head out of the bag.

As we ate our lunch, Susan marked that Kathy must be feeling so much better to be able to keep down that burger.

"Thank you?" remarked Kathy a little hesitantly, as we both looked at Susan strangely.

"Oh, before I forget, I have several boxes of baby clothes that I would love to offer you, if you're interested."

THE BACKSTABBER

Kathy's face wrinkled as she asked Susan why she thought that she was pregnant.

"Oh, Mandy told us," Susan exclaimed. "But she said that you were just at the beginning and very sick so not to say anything. I thought it was okay to speak to you about it, though."

Some of you still may not get it, so let me clue you in on what it was like in the corporate world in the 1980s. Not all women who went out on maternity leave returned to work. Additionally, women with children were viewed as not working as hard as men or women with no children.

"What else did Mandy share," I chimed in.

"Well, she said how you hated the job and was looking for a way out, and you applied for another position, then found out that you were pregnant."

My mouth was now agape as I shook my head from left to right.

Although Kathy told Susan that she wasn't pregnant, the damage was already done. In the long run, it was Mandy who got that other position, regardless of the attempts made to set the story straight. We'll never know if it was because of her skill set or because of the false rumors Mandy spread around the office that got her the job instead of Kathy. The only upside was that she was no longer directly working with us, which made it easier for Kathy to move forward.

Understanding a Backstabber

It took me years to discern the reason why people become backstabbers and this instance was one of many that helped solidify my definition.

Distrust in themselves and their own abilities push backstabbers to build themselves up in the eyes of others, by knocking others down, like a child's game of blocks. This behavior may stem from the way *they* were treated in those impressionable years of their childhood.

They believe that the only way that they can rise is by making others look bad. What they do not know is that in the long run, your candle does not burn brighter when you attempt to extinguish another's.

Dealing with a Backstabber

Over the years with the plethora of people trying to gain another rung in the corporate ladder, I've dealt with my fair share of backstabbers.

Knowing the true nature of this individual does not make it much easier to have compassion for them, especially if you fall victim to their knife.

Kathy was such a kind soul and never let this situation get under her skin. I believe that was the reason that it wasn't long before an even better opportunity presented itself. Kathy applied and got it. She confessed that in the long run it was that second opportunity that was best for her career.

Years later she laughed about it, sending thanks through the airwaves to Mandy, now no longer with the firm.

THE BACKSTABBER

Anyone who stabs you in the back doesn't deserve to be in your life. The key here is to act as Kathy did with Mandy: Forgive, release and move on.

THE SOUTHERN BITCH

Come on now, we've all have had the opportunity to work with someone who has the personality of being the Bitch. Yes, this is typically associated with women, but is not mutually exclusive.

The southern Bitch is a special breed, always sweet to your face as they do their best to mess you up behind your back. If no one else is around, they'll take that opportunity to show their real side.

They use terms like bless your little heart, which is really code for Fuck you very much!

I was on an assignment in a southern state where I experienced a great example of this personality. Let's call her Hilly. She was in the role of a PM and her direct report, Kall, spent about half of my first day with me explaining the organization and structure of the work, as I wrote notes in a notepad, my work PC not yet ready.

I was hopeful that since we were all from the same consulting firm that the three of us would all forge a good working relationship. I receive my PC halfway through my second day, spending an hour with Kall to share with me the links to the internal sites that I needed to access.

Hilly confronted me at the end of that second day after everyone had left, raising her voice to me, stating that I was monopolizing Kall's time and that she was reigning him back in now. She proceeded to chastise me with small digs thrown at my lack of professionalism and ability to come up to speed. I cocked my head puzzled, since I had only been on the job for 2 days.

Understanding the Southern Bitch
They are spiteful and vengeful, but make sure it comes across in a package of southern charm.

Dealing with the Southern Bitch
Take every nicety that they throw your way and believe nothing. Just knowing that whatever comes out of their mouth is only for the benefit of the crowd and that secretly they do not wish you well, will help you deal with this personality.

THE BOMBSHELL/CASANOVA

Anyone who has heard of Marilyn knows what I'm referring to when I mention the word Bombshell. And if you're a fan of middle age history, then you're probably familiar about my reference to the Casanova. When I talk about these personalities, do not assume that it's all flowers and perfume. Actually these people work their charms on both men and women to get what they need.

They do not necessarily need to be overly attractive, but do carry themselves in a way that invites attention. I'll never forget this guy, Mr. Grey that worked in our department. I know what some of you are thinking. No, this was way before the *50 Shades* book, and his first name was not Christian. He was however, filled with mystery and intrigue in most aspects of his life, in and outside the office, verified by many single women in several departments.

For Mr. Grey, women were mere conquests to help him rise to the top. Funny how he seemed to align himself with the highest ranking females throughout the firm, although every single female I spoke with seemed to have a crush on him.

It was Mindy that he ended up aligning himself with, her being 3 levels up from his own. I would find out later that he told her that he was fascinated with what she was doing for the firm. She was so in love with him that she taught him everything she knew, completed some of his assignments and continually recommended him for promotions as he rose within the firm.

I was not surprised when Mr. Grey dumped Mindy the day after he was promoted to the same as her.

The bombshell personality is pretty much the same, with women like this incredibly attractive girl Patty, using her *assets* to get what she needed from the men at the office. At the watercooler, she was the girl most hated by all the other women. She was also the one with the most dates from the pool of the firms' bachelors.

Understanding the Bombshell and Casanova
It's not difficult to peg the reasons why people use their sensuality to rise in the corporate ranks. They feel that that is all they have to offer. Take Mr. Grey for instance. He was incredibly smart, but deep down lacked the self-esteem to be judged solely by his efforts, using his looks and charisma instead to get ahead and get others to help him with his deliverables.

Dealing with the Bombshell and Casanova
When interacting with this personality, I view them as a small child looking for validation, not succumbing to their charms. I am always courteous and provide guidance, but as in life, everyone has to do their own homework, or at the office complete their own work assignments in order to move forward.

THE CLIQUE

Every office, group or business unit has a few individuals that make up the office clique. This may be as little as 2 or as many as 20. They've worked together for years and are determined to hold onto their little kingdom.

They tend to act with arrogance, criticism, cruelty, jealousy, judgment, worry, envy or disdain to outsiders. Anyone who they have to work with who is not in their group is considered an outsider, even those who work under the same manager.

Some call the above, negative emotions. I call them fear based emotions, and they're a cancer that can spread throughout an *organ-ization*.

This is one of the worst groups to work with if you're a consultant, because the clique is threatened by the abilities of anyone outside the clique, believing that you're after their job or there to upset the status quo that they've created.

I'll never forget when I did a private consulting gig for one of the largest pharmaceutical companies in the world. I packed a couple of bags and drove 17 hours across Arizona to a small town in the middle of Texas. I was scheduled to be there for 6 months. My role was to come up with the current state for many systems, then perform gap analysis and provide recommendations for enhancements.

This dark-haired Italian with a NY accent in a suit stood out in an office filled with union staff, where the dress code was jeans every day. My interactions with them were minimal for this assignment. All I needed from them was an account set up, password and the names of certain directories.

I spent my days, headphones on, soft music filling my ears, as I concentrated on my tasks. It was a slow start as I waited for what seemed like forever to get access to the 17 systems I needed to analyze.

It was one morning when I realized that I was getting the full flavor of the office clique, Texas style. That day when the batteries on my MP3 player died, it became apparent that my slow access was due to *the clique*. They were oblivious as I sat there calmly listening to every word from the surrounding cubicles as they plotted.

It ranged from comments like:

"If that consultant thinks that they're going to take my job, they have another thing coming,"

"Oh, I'll never give that consultant the password to that system."

I gave them about 20 minutes, then rose from my cubicle with the headphones still around my ears, the wire dangling at my side.

"By the way, ladies," I said in a cool, non-threatening voice, "just because the headphones are on, doesn't mean the music is playing, so let me get one thing straight. I'm a consultant, that's what I do. The faster you provide me with the information I need, like access and passwords to these systems, the quicker I will be done with my work and out of here."

After that, they never bothered me again.

I've dealt with many a clique in my time. They remind me of those groups when we were in high school, the cool kids who had the great parties that most of us were not invited to.

Understanding the Clique
Know that the groups of people that are the perpetrators of this bad behavior are just insecure. **They're just positioning their group for control.**

Dealing with the Clique
Instead of reacting and allowing your feelings to move toward a corresponding fear based emotion type, if you look on these people with compassion, then you'll be happier and healthier.

Show others the strong fiber you're made of and take the higher road!

I'm not saying that you should be a doormat by any means. You can be an incredibly nice and giving person, but when the clique tries to interfere with your productivity, don't be afraid to show them what you're made of, and that you're a force to be reckoned with.

Just do it without stooping to their level and acting out of fear or anger.

There's more to life than the 8 hours a day we spend in an office setting. Instead of reacting and allowing your feelings to move toward a corresponding fear based emotion, look on these people with compassion.

You'll be happier and healthier if you do.

THE CONTROLLED BURNER

While working in Manhattan, I remember Laura, a young professional who seemed so very nice to everyone she met. She was one of the managers of a group of recent young college grads, all of us green and impressionable.

But Laura had a secret. She was overwhelmed and afraid of being found out as she coped the best she could with all the young talent that she was asked to manage.

I'll never forget the games that she played with the people under her. In her position of authority she yielded so much power, yet it was her inability to realize her strength that kept her from rising any further.

Sean and I were happy co-workers and office mates working side by side for months, sharing an office and having a stellar working relationship. We were more like an old married couple, becoming fixtures in each other's lives, as we provided each other on advice from everything from potential dates to décor, before getting transferred under Laura.

Laura certainly had an interesting management style, never having group meetings, but calling us into her office privately, spending about 30 minutes behind closed doors with us both a few times a week.

I would like to say that it was a time filled with productive conversation about my work performance and how I could improve, but actually I was already a pretty productive worker and outside these schedule times with Laura, I maintained that productivity.

So what was shared with me behind closed doors?

Well, with me, Laura mostly shared some of her disappointment with Sean's performance, "Thanks for picking up the slack for that good-for-nothing office mate of yours. If he doesn't watch out, he will find himself out of a job."

I would later come to understand that line of conversation was inappropriate in the workplace, since a manager should never discuss the performance of another, especially someone on that same level to a subordinate. But I was in my early 20's and knew no better.

After a couple of months, I started to notice a difference in Sean's behavior toward me. All of a sudden he didn't want to hang out after work, nor did he want to have lunch together. Even though we shared an office, he made it a point to avoid me whenever possible.

"So man, what's going on?" I cornered him one day.

"You have a lot of nerve telling management that you're picking up the slack for me and I should be canned," he fired back at me.

He could tell that the look on my face was utter astonishment as I calmly responded, "Sean, I know exactly where you heard that, Laura."

We spent the next few days comparing notes as we discovered what she had done. I was so happy that after all that was said and done I had not lost my good friend.

Understanding a Controlled Burner
This personality feels as if they have absolutely no control in their life. It's very possible that they were abused as children, perhaps having very controlling verbally abusive parents or authority figures. Most people with this personality are mousier in appearance and demeanor. They tend to be soft spoken and tend to pit 2 strong personalities against each other.

A Controlled Burner likes to fuel controversy in a controlled burn sort of way, by carefully choosing their victims and watching them duke it out. It's the epitome of control. They use this kind of chaos creation by coming in and saving the day when a situation they create gets heated, pulling the strings, like a puppet master.

Dealing with a Controlled Burner
If this happens to you, the first thing you can do is confront the person directly, like I did with Sean. As far as jointly confronting the controlled burner, that depends on their position in the firm. Since Lauren was a lower level manager and not a very strong personality, it was not a risk to our positions to jointly confront her and tell her how we felt about what she was doing.

We did it with compassion, as we carefully worked together, choosing our words before meeting with her. We told her that we didn't want there to be any bad feelings, but we no longer would attend private meetings with her. The hope was that it would allow her to work on her behavior. In our case Laura left the firm shortly thereafter, but it was still the right course of action to take.

Remember that when dealing with this personality that specifically pits 2 co-workers against each other in a controlled burn sort of way, that keeping your cool is the key to successfully navigating toward safety and resolution.

THE CREDIT STEELER

Have you ever done the lion's share of work on a project only to have someone else swoop in and get the credit?

I can think of several instances in my career where this has happened. The right course of action is different depending on your role relative to the person who is taking credit.

Same Level

I remember one instance in particular where a co-worker was taking credit for my work for a series of research and development deliverables. Seeking peer feedback I would pass my ideas over to him to get his thoughts, not knowing that he was handing them in as his own.

What I did not know at the time is that people who steel, do this are blinded by a false sense of entitlement. This is similar to greed.

Management

I used to work for a manager who pushed all his deliverables on my plate, in addition to what I was accountable for, only to take the credit for my work product.

After a long 6 month stretch of me doing both mine and his job, I found out via an announcement that he was promoted.

I spent the next weekend sick to my stomach before getting very angry. *'How dare he get promoted, when I was doing all the work,'* I thought.

I tossed and turned at night, in turmoil about my next move. I was so upset I thought about quitting. *'I'll show them,'* I calculated, when I don't show up on Monday.

But who would that serve?

No one. No, it wasn't fair that someone else was taking credit for my work product and getting promoted on top of that to boot. But if I quit, then the only person I was spiting was myself.

Justifiably it is normal to lose respect for someone when they present your work product as their own.

Is it fair? No it's not. But it's also a valuable lesson to stay in your lane. By that I mean that you should only perform the tasks that are specific to your job title and not allow management to push their tasks on you.

Understanding the Credit Stealer
The credit stealer is another personality building themselves up on the backs of others. Although their behavior may be deemed by some as unethical, it's not illegal when dealing with unpatented materials.

In the example of the co-worker, I provided them with the information that they turned in as their own. In the situation of my manager, I was angry for weeks until I stepped back to look at the bigger picture. In this instance, *I* was the one who allowed him to dump his work on me.

Dealing with the Credit Stealer
When faced with a co-worker taking credit for your work, keep your ideas to yourself when in those one-on-one conversations, saving them to share with a larger group. You'll be happy you waited as you receive the credit you richly deserve.

When dealing with a manager who continually attempts to push their work onto you, find the balance between your work and home life, and do not to accept more than you can handle.

In my case, the pattern was already in place and there was no turning back. I took the only course of action that I could, and that was to find a new position within the organization. I was gracious as I left my old position and went into a different department, ensuring that I provided a good transition of my work to the others on my old team.

Funny, but no one else on my old team took on the manager's tasks and they fell back to him. Shortly thereafter, as my old manager floundered, the true nature of who was actually running that department came to light.

As for me, I was quickly promoted under my new management.

THE DISTRACTOR

The distractor, does just that, they do things that are meant to distract and deflect.

This personality will do anything to divert attention away from themselves and any work that they been assigned, even to perform the simplest of tasks. They do this by asking for more details, slice levels, or specific sub task assignments, or countless additional meetings for more clarification. After all the resource time spent, they turn around and push the assignment on to another team entirely, stating that it's not their job.

Do you know anyone like this on your projects are at your company?

These are the people that will put a project in red status!

I was managing a project team where I had a very difficult time in getting the project to move forward. It was on that project that I was first introduced to the distractor in the form of a woman named Natasha.

Within my decades of project management experience, I've rarely dealt with this personality to such a degree that nothing was accomplished for an extended period of time.

As a project manager it makes us look inefficient.

I have also dealt with the distractor personality in the form of a technical project lead for a large initiative, named Rahul. At the time, I was the PM over testing, coming into the project already in progress. After onboarding, I did my typical due diligence, allowing myself to gather all the tasks that my teams needed to perform to support the project. I was taken aback at executive meetings to hear Rahul spewing comments that testing was making the technical side of the project red.

Rahul had the ear of executives, who now look to me for answers.

I was confused after these initial calls, since the project was still in the planning phase and development had not yet begun.

Once I created a detailed timeline that would prove that we were not the cause of any delay, Rahul sited another area that was causing this issue. The actual real issue was that Rahul was put in a position that was way over his abilities. The only way he knew to get through it was to be the personality I call the distractor.

Understanding the Distractor
Like the magician, distractors divert people's attention.

Some even enjoy spending time directing people in continual circles over accomplishing anything.

Knowing that the distractor is trying to gain control by misdirection is the first step. Understand that the reason someone acts this way is usually because they're afraid that they cannot perform the task. Their actions are the same, diverting, stalling, running everyone in circles and perhaps finally pushing the task outside their sphere of influence.

Dealing with the Distractor

While having compassion for this personality that obviously does not understand that there is no 'I' in team, do not give up your power. Do not allow the distractor to frustrate you.

Escalating to their management is the final step, but may not be necessary if you ensure that you remain organized and concise as an action to gain back control.

THE FINGER POINTER

Don't you just love to hate the finger pointer? These are the people who will throw you under the bus when the shit hits the fan, as they conspire to make sure none of it sticks to them. I have seen senior staff position themselves in such a way, that when the boom is lowered, they can come out of it unscathed.

I have been fortunate not to have to deal with a lot of finger pointing in my career, where the finger was pointed my way, but I can tell you that I have seen a ton of it pointed to teams and individuals that were not at fault.

One example comes to mind relative to a project where I had the opportunity to work with a fellow consultant named Karl, who wore his previous achievements like a badge of honor, spewing to anyone who would listen how great he was. Unfortunately, there was little if nothing else that he actually accomplished. When the project failed, Karl was the first to blame every other manager on the project for their lack of cooperation. The good thing for the rest of us is that we had our deliverables dated and saved in the project's document repository. When upper management analyzed this earthquake of a project, it was obvious where the fault lay. Once it was evident, Karl quickly changed his tune, pointing the fickle-finger of blame toward the staff he was managing. That also turned out to be a bust for him, since this staff also kept good records of what they were assigned. In the end, all fingers pointed back to this Karl's inabilities. All the self-aggrandizing in the world did not save him from the axe.

If Karl was in over his head, he could have asked for assistance, but instead, he was so pumped-up drinking his own cool-aide that he let it cloud the fact that he was playing with fire.

Understanding the Finger Pointer
Know that finger pointing is done out of fear of reprisal, reputation and loss of job security, so it is no wonder why it is not uncommon in the workplace.

Dealing with the Finger Pointer
Unlike the example provided, people who are experts at finger pointing, sometimes do get away with it. My advice is to ensure that what you are doing is well-organized, properly documented and dated. In short, cover your *ASSets* and don't worry about the finger pointers of this world. Karma eventually gives them exactly what they deserve!

THE GASLIGHTER

If you're an old movie buff, then you may be familiar with a movie from 1944 named Gaslight, starring Ingrid Bergman and Charles Boyer.

Wikipedia defines gaslighting as a form of mental abuse in which information is twisted or spun, selectively omitted to favor the abuser, or false information is presented with the intent of making victims doubt their own memory, perception, and sanity.

The people portraying such forms of what I term deceptive mind manipulation, are at a minimum, sociopaths to borderline and full out psychopaths.

Okay, so I really need to be crude here to drive home the essence of this personality. These folks are the ultimate mind-fuck.

Of all the personalities that I describe in this book, this personality is the one to watch out for.

I find it amazing how these sociopaths to borderline psychopaths can actually function, interact and fit themselves into the workplace. They may come across as your best friend or having your best interest at heart to win your confidence, then act on the information you've shared to use it against you to throw you off guard, until you question your every action.

Understanding the Gaslighter

It really depends on the individual, with the hardest one to deal with in direct management to you. They can come on strong right from the start, be your best friend, or just be totally aloof at first, waiting patiently until they are ready to pounce. And believe me, they will.

Why? Most commonly it's because controlling and manipulating people is exactly what they do to hide something lacking in themselves. The first thing they do is make sure that they keep you close to them, so you're never out of their sphere of control. They'll isolate you in whatever way they can, ensuring what they tell you can be contradicted when you are in a public setting.

For example, let's say that you begin a position in a new company. They can tell you something negative about each and every person that's in your department as well as ancillary departments that you have to work with, ensuring that you're leery about making friends and building new relationships. They may try and control you by ensuring that absolutely every piece of correspondence or bit of information has to come through them. Listen darlings, there are a ton of ways to control and manipulate people at the workplace. And the gaslighter knows them all!

A perfect example I experienced with a gaslighter was at one of my technical consulting assignments. Steven, my direct manager was definitely a borderline psychopath, fully adept at the technique of gaslighting. It was less than 2 weeks at the assignment when I realized that I was in a state of panic. This was not like me at all. It started with a couple of instances of misdirection, sending me to the wrong person, who had no idea why I was coming to them for information. When I questioned Steven, the answer I received was that they never told me to talk to person X or person Y. I knew what I was told, so I chalked it up to the fact that he must have been overwhelmed. It escalated to indecisiveness, then direction switching, then to all out lying about my responsibilities, telling me that I would be taking over the management of a small team of 6 that currently reported to another person, and that the announcement of the new responsibility would come at the next meeting. I scheduled my first meeting with this new group, finding out later that these 6 were never intended to be under me. Shortly thereafter, I was invited to participate in a meeting with one of my peer managers with whom I would be closely working. I was blindsided as the manager started off the meeting belligerently, professing that they needed to explain to us our role on the project. In that meeting they explained that the workload had changed and there was a possibility that one of us would be let go.

The workload of this assignment *was* small in comparison to some of the mega projects I had managed in the past, so I felt little to no stress. Someone potentially effecting my wallet, however, would stress anyone out. I was left there in a panic the remainder of the week as I jumped to attention at the slightest little thing.

I had to ask myself what was truly going on here. As I sat home one evening, I felt the need to write down all that had transpired within that first few weeks. As I looked at the statistics, an article about gaslighting surfaced. It was then that I put 2 and 2 together as it dawned on me, who exactly I was dealing with.

Once I realized that Steven was a gaslighter, my behavior changed, and other things came to light. As I sat there listening to Steve in meetings, I realized that whenever anyone asked him a question, his answer was always, "That's not important right now." With over 30 years of experience under my belt, I started to see things more clearly, and realized that perhaps part of his form of gaslighting.

You see, once you know what a spade looks, sounds and acts like, it's easier not to allow yourself to react. Knowing who I was dealing with was 90% of the battle. It was not long, that I was able to do my best to work, preferring to work around this manager.

Unfortunately, that was not the only Gaslighter that I've dealt with in my career. On one assignment I worked with Hans, who seemed to be a very jovial fellow. Advanced in years, he always wore a smile. I will never be sure if it was the signs of early senility or gaslighting that had him discussing one topic with me, then switching gears to do the opposite of what we chatted about, only to state that we never spoke. It was an assignment where I never seemed to accomplish anything, the back and forth exchanges taking all of my time.

Dealing with a Gaslighter

I would love to tell you that there's an easy way to deal with a manager who is also one of these personalities. Unfortunately, the only thing that you can do is not react to them, keep good notes and do the best you can.

These people are just too far down the rabbit hole for redemption.

The more common action is to try and get as far away from them as possible. Leave the department if you can, planning your exit strategy accordingly.

THE INFORMATION WITHHOLDER

Ah, those who either withhold information, trying to gain some sense of control over their own life or purposing trickling information in an attempt to control others.

For the Information Withholder, they are the people that will tell you almost everything about a process, situation or job function, but leave out a crucial piece that ties it all together. They're like that relative, you know the one who shares with you that recipe, leaving out one of the ingredients. The moment you ask a question or two for clarification, instead of being provided with a direct answer they send you off into another direction. I don't know about you, but I'm not fond of the wild goose chase. They communicate to others their surprise that you just don't get it, relishing in your utter frustration.

Information withholders usually come off as delicate but don't be fooled. They're not overwhelmed and they know exactly what they're doing. When I think of this sort of person, I think about a manager I once had named Mary. She was a frail woman who was as savvy as they come, soft spoken, but deadly.

And then there was Dillon, a peer analyst I worked with in a contract in the south. As he handed off some of his current in-flight projects to me, the new consultant, he conveniently left out main key pieces of information. It was not long before I realized that I did not have everything that I needed to succeed.

Understanding the Information Withholder
This personality has a desire to feel superior over others, leaving those in their wake totally exasperated.

This personality can take the form of someone who trickles information, to a true information withholder, that if you attempt to reach out to someone outside of the 2-by-2 of your cubicle, you get slapped back down into the abyss, licking your wounds.

Dealing with the Information Withholder
The key is understanding why they feel the need to control the information they're dispensing. Continue to organize your work, ideas and steps to ask direct questions on a process. If you do this, the information withholder has no choice but to answer your questions, providing you the missing piece of the puzzle, that *golden ticket* that will get you to the next level.

THE MISFIT

Every time I hear the word misfit, I think about that holiday cartoon from my youth, the one filled with the land of misfit toys. In reality, the misfit is the team member who seems to all to be in over their head, not being able to do anything right.

They'll reach out to anyone who'll help them, hiding their lack of knowledge, telling their management that they have not been provided with any information as a stall tactic.

Unfortunately, they expend their own and others time as they ask the same questions over and over to different audiences until everyone tires of the continual spoon feeding they provide to them with no positive result.

It was a decade ago when I dealt with Teresa, a young project manager, who epitomized the role of the Misfit. It was obvious that this gal had no real desire to be a PM, taking the position after a re-shift of roles after a company downsize.

Teresa elicited the help of several senior PMs to help her, each of us taking several hours per week to mentor her. It was not until I compared notes with one of my peers did I realize that we were both being asked the same set of questions and providing the same set of deliverable templates and walk-throughs to this gal.

That sparked us to ask Teresa who else she was going to for assistance. In the end we found out that Teresa was asking a total of 5 project managers for assistance, each of us providing her with the same information.   After 6 month's we collectively decided to perform an analysis of Teresa's skill set. She did not improve.

Understanding the Misfit

The misfit personality begins early in childhood. They're afraid of failure and take little risks because of their lack of confidence, their whole life having been one scary experience after another.

As a child they were most likely not at the top of their class, the last to get picked for dodgeball. In the business world they are the first to get laid off.

The misfit is not unique. They have a hard time assimilating and catching up to others in the workplace. At the office, they're so afraid of getting laid off that they continually feel overwhelmed.

Dealing with the Misfit

As a manager, the best advice I can offer other managers is to show them both a firm hand and compassion as you help them understand the meaning of deadlines, provide them with direction and praise small victories to start building their confidence.

How to Overcome Being the Misfit

If you're the misfit personality, know that you can rid yourself of doubt with a little determination. Doubt is a funny thing. It keeps us from stretching our wings and flying. Think about that little engine Thomas who was known for saying, "I think I can, I think I can." Stop doubting your ability. Instead say to yourself, "I know I can, I know I can!"

You have to change your perspective and believe this strongly. You need to take responsibility for your actions and deliverables and stop beating yourself up for small setbacks. In time you will start feeling a little better. For this personality, a simple strengthening mantra will help you find your strength.

THE OVERACHIEVER

In this segment I speak about the workaholic, that I affectionately call the overachiever. This is the person that you love to hate. In school they were probably the straight A student who set the curve.

Understanding the Overachiever
These people are either driven based on a need for approval. They continually try to prove themselves to gain the recognition and acceptance they didn't received during childhood. Or maybe they're just looking for something to do with their time outside of beer pong.

They are so dedicated to their job that they work with blinders on shutting out everything else in their life.

Most people don't like someone who is an overachiever, but some companies, as part of their strategy, strive to create this type of employee. They do so by isolating them from their normal environment, having them travel outside their home city each week, so they have a captive audience, a working machine. And these employees will work until they drop.

I know a lot about the overachiever, I once was one, working in management and financial services consulting for the first part of my career. In the 1990s I moved from New York to Washington, DC. I was single in a new city and driven to prove myself. With no family and no concept of wanting to leave work, I was all business; heads down with my daily dose of single malt scotch at the Old Ebbitt Grill down the street from the office at 10 each evening after my workday ended.

I received accolades from management and sneers from fellow office mates whose work product was compared to mine.

Dealing with the Overachiever
If you're dealing with an overachiever, I need you to ask yourself a couple of questions: Why are you so bothered by this person? Are they physically or mentally torturing you in some way that has your panties in a bunch?

If it's merely because this person is able to devote more time to the job, then wish them well. Most likely they won't be in your department for very long, because once they master the routine, the sheer boredom of it will have them moving on to the next challenge.

If they want to pick up the slack, let them, while you enjoy a warm setting and a home cooked meal with your family.

How to determine if you're falling into the overachiever trap
Do you think that you may be a workaholic, an overachiever and want to change? Do you continually:

- Have trouble shutting off when you go home?
- Think about work while in bed before you go to sleep?

- Toss and turn at night thinking about an assignment you're working on?
- Think about work first thing in the morning before you get out of bed?
- Believe that work will stop if you take a day off?
- Cancel personal plans due to work?
- Check your emails on weekends and when on vacation?

If the majority of the answers to the questions below are yes most of the time, then you could be an overachiever.

How to Break Overachiever Traits
Take your hands off the keyboard every once in a while and take a moment to think about something other than work.

Take time to enjoy life now. Find your passion. Work is just that, work. It doesn't define you as a person, no matter what you think while you're doing it. In the big scheme of things, it's the people whose lives you touch, who you've loved, that you will be remembered for when you're long gone, not making that deadline.

For years I fit this mold and sacrificed what was important, as I gave all to the job.

I was recently faced with a similar situation. I once again put my best foot forward on a private corporate assignment, finishing something in a few hours that should have taken more than a day to complete. One of the guys commented, "Boy, aren't we the overachiever." It hit a nerve in me, not in anger, but made me take note that I still have work to do, that I'm still a work in progress.

Hopefully this puts things into perspective for you.

THE PESSIMISTIC PANICKER

In life we meet people who worry about this and that. In the workplace they are the gloom and doom naysayers that plague the space with negativity. The sky is always falling, the tank is on empty and the next layoff is a tsunami that's going to sweep everyone away.

Their words leave a wake of sadness and despair as all around them get sucked into the ever growing vortex they create. Just like an optimist can bring team spirit to its apex, the pessimist can bring it to the depths of the abyss.

These folks certainly spoil the holiday party, don't they? You'll notice that as you leave their space you feel drained and maybe a little depressed.

Understanding a Pessimistic Panicker

This personality stems from feelings of continual despair. When you know that a person who is that negative, it usually pervades every aspect of their life. They wear their misery comfortably like a tattered old blanket. This type of personality does not form overnight, it's created after many years of practice, starting early in life.

Dealing with the Pessimist Panicker

Show these people by example how joyous and enriching this existence can be. I've learned that you can lead a horse to the trough, but some people just don't want to drink the Kool-Aid. Alas, if they only knew how delicious life could be if they just got out of their own way.

How to Overcome Being a Pessimistic Panicker

If you have a tendency to be this personality, know that you can change your outlook in an instant. Yes everyone has experiences, both pleasant and unpleasant. It's when we realize that if we identify with the pleasant ones giving them more of our focus that things change for us.

People don't realize that it's just as easy to see the glass filling then emptying.

You have the power to make a difference in your own life. Why not make it a positive change!

THE POWER TRIPPER

Have you ever had to deal with a person in your organization that was so full of themselves on a continual power trip that you have to take a step back and ask why?

Most likely if they are on the same level as you, you can easily ignore them. But what happens when this person is your manager?

I was speaking to my friend Rachel a senior manager with over 20 years of experience working with large corporations. As I patiently listened to her describe her current situation with her boss, it brought me back to a couple of managers I've dealt with since the 1980's. As is typical of the power-tripper personality, Rachel's accounting of her boss included, an over inflated ego and a silo management style.

I could see that this gal had really hit a nerve when Rachel mentioned a conversation where her manager said, *"She belongs to me,"* as she pointed to her when speaking to a peer manager.

"She knew I could hear what she was saying. She does stuff like that to me all the time, but others she treats like gold," she complained, as Rachel went further with the host of items she had endured over the past few years.

Poor Rachel had been dealing with a manager that believed that the best worker was one she could control through limiting the information they were allowed to receive or request. Absolutely everything had to funnel down through her. Then there was the dispensing of continual reprimands when Rachel tried to be proactive and ask questions outside the silo. Rachel cried as she continued explaining that her manager chastised her, discounting her ability to do the job because Rachel acted with more independence than other peer managers.

I've known Rachel for over a decade and I would work with this intelligent, capable, get-the-job-done non-political powerhouse anytime.

Understanding the Power Tripper

It's very difficult dealing with this personality when they hold the purse strings to your performance reviews, raises and bonuses. To outside groups, peer managers or upper management they may come across very sweet and caring. Only the staffers that they decide to show this personality to know the real story, one that has made some of you want to slit your wrists as you continually swallow your pride.

Dealing with the Power Tripper

Know that when interacting with this type of personality, especially when they feel slighted, do so as if you are dealing with a hurt child. Be patient and kind. You see this person really does not have it out for you. They are so unhappy with their own life that they are taking it out on the people with the best energy around them and those who react. By reacting you are only fueling the fire and giving them what they need, power. But in this case it is your power that they are adding to their trip.

If you love your job, but not this type of manager and are asked to swallow your pride, then first determine if it is a wake-up call for you to look within and determine why you're feeling this way. Is it your ego that needs to be in check? If not, and you can stick it out and have as little interaction with this person as possible, then that is my first suggestion.

If you cannot bear dealing with this person, then look for work in another department.

No one should be subjected to someone who builds themselves up by breaking others down.

THE RESCUER

The rescuer almost sounds like the knight in shining armor, coming to the aid of damsels in distress. At the office, the rescuers role is to come in and save the day when crisis befalls a project or department.

If you work in most companies today, it's not hard to imagine the chaos and the need for this personality as they swoop in and do what it takes to turn things around.

They get-off on pressure that would make most others pop. They are incredibly bored when everything is status quo.

And then there are those who make themselves the rescuer by creating situations that they are the only ones that have the key to solve. It's like the theme song from the cartoon, Mighty Mouse, *"Here I come to save the day!"*

Understanding the Rescuer
These are your thrill seekers, who will climb Everest just for kicks. Most would never be caught dead in an office and find vocations where they can utilize their true talents like fighting fires or walking on steel beams at the top of framed skyscrapers.

Many consultants fall into this category, due to the ever changing job circumstances that continually put them in new cities and new situations. Let's face it, consultants come in where there is a lack of expertise or staffing.

Dealing with the Rescuer

Although you're glad and possibly ecstatic for their assistance, these people generally get all the accolades for their heroic efforts, whether they expect it or not. That tends to put people off, since it's always the efforts of the entire team that really help save the day.

Know that most rescuers will move on once they consider the job boring, seeking out the next chaotic project to sink their teeth into.

That may provide you with some comfort when you're dealing with this personality.

THE SABOTEUR

There are many flavors of office sabotage. Some forms of sabotage are perpetrated to make others work life miserable out of sheer meanness, while others in order to rise in an organization.

Mark, a cheerful nurse at a patient rehabilitation center. Marked shared the load of caring for 32 in his unit with another RN, named Amy and a supervisory RN named Charlotte. From the beginning Amy and Mark did not see eye-to-eye on various processes and procedures, but Mark tried his best to work with her. When the facility lost their supervisory RN, Amy was assigned to temporarily fill this role as the facility worked on filling the role. Amy had such distain for Mark she took every opportunity to frustrate him until he quit. First, she continually changed his work schedule in total opposition to his requests.

When Amy discovered that nothing she was doing effected Mark she took it to the next level. At care centers, RN's must complete new patient admission assessments within 24 hours as mandated by the state. Amy instructed Mark to start an assessment for a new patient, promising that she would print and sign it in the morning. Amy never completed the form allowing the 24 hour deadline to pass. When the weekly state audit discovered the oversight Amy was quick to blame it on Mark's incompetence. Mark received a call a couple of days later from the district supervisors stating that he was terminated.

Why would someone do this?

I had an interesting example of sabotage when dealing with a Russian woman that was on the team I was managing in a matrixed organization on one of my assignments. Instead of being a team player, she was destructive, filibustering my teleconference meetings, telling my then management on the calls the many ways that I was incapable. It was one of the most unproductive times in my work life until I determined what was going on.

Understanding the Saboteur
I believe it has to do with one of several fear based emotions like anger, hate and distain that make people behave with such vengeance.

Of all the personalities I mention, this one is the unhappiest in their personal life.

The message for saboteurs is simple:

> **Your candle does not glow brighter by trying to extinguish someone else's**.

Dealing with the Saboteur
In the case of Mark, he handled the situation beautifully, continuing to do his best, staying focused, remaining a team player, all the time knowing Amy's motives. He calmly strolled into his HR appointment the next

morning to hand in his badge. He also brought with him a copy of the dated assessment with Amy's instructions. In the end, he received a good letter of recommendation and was quickly picked up for an even better position. He shared with me that he heard Amy was let go shortly thereafter.

When dealing with sabotage, always take the high road and do your best to keep good records and remain organized. In most cases, their true nature will become apparent to others in the office without your intervention. If you allow your emotions to get the better of you, then the saboteur wins.

EMOTIONAL SABOTAGE

Emotional sabotage takes place, not only in the workplace, but with interactions in our everyday life. I preface this by saying that for the most part people who do this are "unaware" that their words are having this effect on us.

Below are the labels I've given them along with examples that will put them into perspective.

The Tyrant
First there's the Tyrant. This person is intimidating you in some way. On the larger end of the spectrum, recall any episode of the Sopranos, where there is always someone in someone else's face threatening them with bodily harm. Another is road rage.

At the workplace, you don't have to get down and dirty, rolling on the floor to be a victim of intimidation.

I had an interesting example of intimidation when dealing with a stressed out man named Raj on one of my assignments. He cornered one of my then team leads into the men's room, threatening to have he and his whole team fired if they did not go around the established process and give him what he wanted.

The Thousand Questioner
The next type of person can only be described as the person who makes you ask a thousand questions, so you have to continually probe to find out what is really going on with this person. A good example is the person you have to ask 10 questions to find out that they went shopping for a shirt at JC Penney's, when they could have told you that in their first response. Instead, it took 10 minutes to pull that information from them.

Have you ever worked with this type of individual?

The Woe is Me
Now let me describe the person I call the *Woe is Me.* You get a phone call from someone, and as you look at your caller ID, you cringe. You know that you'll be on the phone for at least an hour with this person, as they talk your ear off about all the things that are going wrong. You hesitate to pick up the phone as you take a moment to decide if you have at least an hour to spend. Then the guilt starts, as it has been awhile since you have answered the phone when this person calls and have not yet called them back, so you pick up the phone. This

is difficult if it's a work associate, because you *have* to pick up that phone. As you anticipated, you're on the phone over an hour as they direct the initial conversation toward work, then unload on you about some workplace woe they are personally experiencing. They're usually a very negative person and a continual victim. Everything that can go wrong has gone wrong with them. After they speak to you, they always feel better. That's why they keep coming to you. All of us knows this type of person. When you finally hang up the phone, you feel drained, like you were hit by a truck, exhausted and distracted.

The Bubble Buster

The next person is what I affectionately have named the *bubble buster*. This person knows someone that has done something bigger and better than you have. No matter what good news you share with this work associate, he or she will always find a way to burst your bubble. I'll never forget my excitement about a promotion when I received my first vice presidency. I was so ecstatic, on cloud 9. I rang one of my prior managers to share the news, who instead of congratulating me, promptly informed me that one of my old peers was just promoted as well and that they must be handing out VP titles to just anyone.

Again, this personality comes in many forms in and outside the workplace. In my personal life, my own mother was skilled at the art of busting bubbles. I'll never forget my excitement about replacing my older home's home ratty 70's shag carpet with tile. In phoning my mother to share the good news, the first words out of her mouth was pop my excitement bubble as she told me about a family friend's child who installed something better in their home.

We all know the appropriate response when sharing good news with someone is for them to say, *"Congratulations; that's great news; I am so happy for you."*

However, the bubble-buster will find some way to deflate or pop your balloon or bubble. The worst kind of bubble-buster is the kind that every time you share good news with them, they respond with *must be nice*. These people believe you are rubbing your joy in their face as an affront to them.

The Firestarter

Last is the *Firestarter*. This is a mind game that the perpetrator plays with their potential victims, throwing a verbal grenade or flame into a crowd or at a specific person, then stepping back to watch the flame. The reactions are usually instantaneous but can also be prolonged. One of the managers I worked under for a year, named Edith would continually attempt to get a rise out of me using cleverly placed verbal grenades. One in particular that stands out was in the midst of my busiest times, at the height of my project's work madness. It was shortly after a status call where I received praise from a level above her for coming up with quick resolution to a problem that helped the department. The bomb she dropped was regarding my role possibly going away, 7 ½ months prior to the event happening. She stated that I will have to think about finding a new job. Outside the fact that does nothing to motivate your workforce, corporate decisions change all the time. I have managed many people over the years and a manager never inform their subordinates that they *may* lose their job that far in advance.

Do you know someone in the office that's a fire-starter?

THE SCRAMBLER

Every major department has at least one scrambler. They are the person who justifies their existence by producing output based on calculations put together in such a way as to merely confuse anyone who tries to decipher them.

This holds true in technology, but perhaps you know someone who has a unique filing system, or an interesting way of organizing information. No one can successfully cover for them because even a rocket scientist would have difficulties understanding the logic of what they've put together.

They often complain about how they cannot take a day off, but are secretly proud of the fact that their creation cannot be maintained because of how they've structured it.

Understanding the Scrambler

I've known a few of these unique individuals. They view themselves as highly intelligent, smarter than everyone else since no one can follow their logic. In actuality, they're very unhappy and have little to look forward to in their life, validating their existence based on the mishmash of information. They're typically threatened by anyone with demonstrated intelligence, they are the first to complain and the last to provide resolution.

How to Deal with the Scrambler
Although my first response is to tell you to run the other way, it does no good, especially if you're asked to take over the work of this individual when they're out of the office. Know that it may take many extra hours to unlock their secret code.

I have had to deal with a scrambler before and liken this experience with using the "Rose decipher" in the Da Vinci code. I only had compassion for this person, as I could sense how miserable they must be.

Know that when dealing with the scrambler, take a simple approach with looking at one piece at a time and write notes. This will help you in the long run should you need to cover for them again.

What to do if you are the Scrambler
Scramblers go out of their way to make things more complicated than they have to be. Realizing you're a scrambler is the first step to moving out of this pattern. Waking up to this realization is a gift, a chance to simplify your work life as well as your home life. I'm not surprised when I meet a scrambler and find out that their home is cluttered, their bills unorganized and their checkbooks a mess.

De-cluttering and simplification are the keys to gaining more control and peace. Everyone at home and the office will appreciate the change

.

THE SCREAMER

I think over our careers we've all dealt with at least one screamer. This person seems incredibly angry at something and will scream about it in the office, on the phone, via voice mail, etc. You know who I am talking about, don't you?

I remember when I was asked to create a daily report to top executives for someone who was out on vacation. I was instructed to take all the information and plug it in exactly as it was provided and not to deviate. After a few decades in the corporate arena I have a reputation of delivering work, based on best practices for excellence, so when I received the information I took the time to read it to understand the overall picture. In doing so I discovered flaws in the instructions that I was provided and had to slightly tweak the report to represent the true nature of the current status.

Although I received recognition from management for the most concise report they've received in years, that wasn't the response from the screamer, who was so angry at me for not blindly listening. In this instance, they even told me to change it back to the way they had it, citing the potential backlash they may receive, even though management, the folks that would provide this backlash were thrilled with the improvement. After the tongue lashing I received, they emailed me and blew up my cell with continual berating texts. I was consulting on that assignment, so there was little I could do to complain about their behavior.

Understanding the Screamer
Screamers are people filled with anxiety. They react out of anger at anyone and everyone that's in their space. Knowing that the anger a screamer demonstrates is not really directed at you may help. It certainly has helped me when dealing with this personality.

Dealing with the Screamer
In the instance I cited, instead of getting angry with the person for their bad behavior, I explained to them that although I provide my clients with what they need, I cannot in my heart send out work that I know is incorrect. Standing up to a screamer without actually stooping to their level is the best way to handle this personality. Here's the difference. I approached the situation with compassion to dispel their anger. The outcome was eventually well received and the screamer apologized to me.

What if you're the screamer?
If you're a screamer, first I want to point out that old saying, *"You get more flies with honey then vinegar."*

No one wants to work with such an unreasonable person. If you're interested in changing your behavior, one of the first things you can do is identify the root cause of your anger. You know that the root has nothing to do with work. It's most likely something in your personal life from the past that you've not yet dealt with and released. I've been working in alternative healing modalities for years and can share they there are many ways to identify, process and release old hurts.

THE SEED PLANTER

Imagine a person dressed in gardening regalia, darning floppy hat and padded gloves, potting mix in tow. Although these seed planters share with the common gardener the ability to plant seeds that grow, the types of seeds that *they* plant are totally different. You see the gardener sows their seeds in fields. And the seed planter sows their seeds in rumors.

Just think about the influence that social media has today and you know what I am talking about. Your yard plots filled with rich soil, yielding beautiful blooms, tall trees or nourishing fruits and vegetables. Conversely, these seed planters in the office sow their seeds in the minds of their associates in attempts to sour and spoil their targeted terrain.

I recall a perfect example of this type of behavior when my friend Vicki sought my council back in the 1980's. She was living in an apartment searching for her first home and found the perfect place. She was on cloud 9 as she described this place to her friends, family and co-workers; that is until she encountered the office rumor mill. I was shocked when I saw her a couple of days later, her eyes glazed over.

"What's going on?" I asked, as I looked upon Vicki's energy wondering what steamroller she had encountered.

She sat on the sofa and broke down, tears streaming down her face, not able to speak. I comforted her, bringing her through a couple of calming techniques until her breathing was back to normal.

"I can't buy that house," she whimpered with great sorrow.

"Why not? Did the owners back out of the deal?" I asked.

"No, no, nothing like that. There may be a big lay-off coming at work and my department will be the first that is hit," she gasped.

"Well, breathe and let me take a moment to help you figure this out," I replied.

I cocked my head as I turned to her asking, "Vicki, can I ask how you know this?"

"Oh, well, one of my co-workers gave me the scoop on this one," she confessed.

I knew at this point, either the information was valid or just a seed planter doing what they do best, planting seeds of doubt as it relates to something in the workplace. I decided to find out which to help my friend.

I took her hand and inquired, "Vicki, how reliable is the information that this person has provided to you. Are they in the management stream or in the meetings where these decisions are made? Are they married to or best friends with these people where they would receive this inside information?"

"Well, no."

"So what makes you think that the information they are providing is reliable and accurate?"

Vicki sat there bewildered, yet began to come to the realization that her worrying may have not had any foundation.

I rose and walked toward the kitchen expressing, "Yes, I'm going to leave you and allow you to let that sink in for a few minutes."

Eventually the corners of her mouth formed a smile that changed to a frown, then a grimace of frustration as she hollered for my return. "Why would someone do that?"

"If you're asking why someone after you have told them the most fabulous news would go out of their way to make someone else believe that a terrible event will occur, it happens all the time."

Understanding the Seed Planter
Seed planters are not thrill seekers. Quite the opposite, they're more content to sit on the sidelines and watch the game. They worry too much about most everything, but they're not victims, since they have no empathy. They actually relish opportunities to point out the possible negative outcomes of situations, gaining for them the same sense of power from performing this technique as one would from leading an organization.

Dealing with the Seed Planter
My best advice is to let their words roll, like water off a ducks back. They have no validity and certainly no power, unless of course you give their words power.

THE TOE STEPPER

Not to be confused with someone who is specifically assigned to assist in some area where there may be overlap, the toe stepper personality is just what you would expect, someone encroaching on your world in the workplace.

They come into your department and not only do their job, but start doing yours without invitation or assignment.

I remember Joe, who joined my department when I worked in Manhattan. The man would get in at dawn and was there well past the time that we all left. He created new ways for us to organize our data and reports, then started grabbing small sections of work assigned to the other 8 people on the team, something that angered my fellow team mates.

Understanding the Toe Stepper
In reality, they're most likely clueless, driven workers, who solely have a need to achieve and probably not much life outside of work.

Dealing with the Toe Stepper
There are a couple of ways to approach the situations that the toe stepper creates. You can either allow them to take some of your work burden from you, especially if you are overwhelmed, or you can set clear boundaries. My suggestion in setting boundaries is to

schedule time to speak to them after you have a chance to take the emotion out of it.

In Joe's case, once the team set the boundaries of each of our work products, the toe stepping behavior stopped. I took Joe out to lunch afterward to see how he was feeling after the meeting. Joe never intentionally tried to step on anyone's toes, he was new and just trying to prove his worth.

Never let the Toe Stepper at work get to you. Remember your reaction is always within your control.

THE VICTIM

Every large department has someone who has a victim personality. It's easy to identify this person because they feel that everyone is against them. They gain the energy of the entire staff as they continually become someone who, based on the way they tell it, is taken advantage of by management, co-workers, vendors, other departments and so on. In their personal life they fall victim to their family and community.

I worked in the same firm with Susan. We lived in neighboring towns and became friends outside of work. At first I was continually consoling her about the supposed *abuse* she was receiving from her manager. We worked for the same manager, so I found it a little strange that she was being mistreated, since I thought the manager was amazing.

The stories she would tell were so damming that I said to her one day that if she felt this way, she should speak to HR and make a formal complaint. She never did, but transferred departments instead.

Then it was the co-worker who she accused of sabotaging her work, the girlfriend of another co-worker who was stalking her, and the list goes on.

I remember the time I took off work to meet her at the courthouse where she obtained a restraining order against an ex-boyfriend who she claimed had threatened her life. From there I rented a truck on her behalf, helped her move her stuff out of their shared apartment into a storage unit.

Over that 10-year period we were friends, I saw a pattern of the victim personality; and it was continual.

Understanding the Victim
The victim is looking for attention, most likely not feeling ignored when they were younger. Some people gain the attention they seek by acting out, showboating, over exaggerating situations or just plain making stuff up. The victim gains it by playing the role of damsel or in distress, even if they are men.

Dealing with the Victim
If someone is truly being victimized at the workplace, you want to help them in any way you can. If you determine that you're dealing with a victim, knowing that the root cause is just their need for attention can help you formulate a more appropriate response. Sometimes, the best course of action is to look on them with empathy and acknowledge the information, but take no action. Once the victim realizes that you're not going to be their knight in shining armor, they'll stop coming to you with their latest dilemma.

That may sound cruel, but if you continually come to the aid of their self-created drama, then you're creating a co-dependent relationship. I know you don't want that!

SECTION 2 – THE CORPORATE DYNAMIC

In this section I describe the corporate dynamic that has morphed over past decades into what it is today.

Again, I emphasize that it is what it is.

When we don't take it personally we're better equipped to deal with what's thrown at us in healthier ways.

THE CORPORATE EVOLUTION

For as long as the elders in our families have shared stories with us, in the past, people typically worked for one company for most of their career. They started with a firm right out of high school or college, worked for approximately 40 years, then retired with, if they were fortunate, a pension. The entire company was one big extended family with people concerned about each other.

Yes there was stress related to jobs, but there was more joy being part of this workforce, shown in their productivity as well as their interactions with their co-workers, family, friends and society.

I believe this dynamic allowed the workforce to concentrate their efforts on performing their jobs, creating new and better products and processes. They had little to worry from the fear of termination due to other than poor performance. Of course there are exceptions to every rule, evidenced by worldwide unemployment during periods of great economic strife, like the Great Depression.

Then came the years that some of the baby-boomers experienced, me being one of them. Oh, I remember those days when I first entered the corporate arena, where long client lunches were the norm. At the suggestion of my first manager, I learned to drink single malt scotch. I was barely 20 when we went out to lunches with the client, the single malts generously poured. I sat there milking mine with a continual water back while I watched and learned. That was indeed a long time ago, when one was expected to drink alcohol at a client lunch meeting, if your client was also drinking. Back then a cigar aficionado was able to smoke portions of the 3 varieties of cigars he had with him at the table, like intermezzos in between courses.

Times were indeed very different back then, where my bosses would brag about their $20,000 monthly expense stipend. That bought us lavish meals at Sam and Harry's, the Old Ebbitt Grill, the Union Oyster House or Musso and Frank's, depending on the part of the country the client was located. The hotels where we stayed were just as well appointed, their elaborate chandeliers opulent centerpieces, augmenting the richness of their over-the-top décor.

It was a great time to be in the corporate arena, knowing that the next meal you ate was going to tantalize your senses.

Things started to change for most middle managers somewhere into the 1990's, as corporations began to crack down on spending for certain levels of management. I still wonder why things changed. Maybe it was due to advances in technology that allowed firms to go global. Or perhaps it was due to the decade plus of takeovers, mergers and hostile acquisitions.

Since then I've seen companies restructured many times, continually figuring out new and better ways to provide quality work as they squeeze the most out of every dollar spent to keep stock prices rising.

I believe that comes at a cost, as it seems that some firms today no longer show their workers the loyalty they did in the past.

Creating an environment centered on fear of termination for reasons other than poor performance, sparks a workforce mindset that's no longer centered on performance. If you ask most people today, especially in certain industries, their prime deliverable has shifted to their paycheck, since they now focus part of their time thinking about whether or not they'll have a job tomorrow and how to provide for their families. This new dynamic based on fear yields less quality deliverables for companies.

Can any of you imagine what it's like to go to work most days with the fear of being let go?

I can almost see some of you that are reading this book, shaking your head yes.

I have worked in some of those companies, were you're in meetings with dozens of people in the morning and by lunch time, they are no longer there. Without time to transfer knowledge and work in progress to existing staff, they are marched out the door as part of the firm's decision to cut workforce numbers. That leaves increasing workloads on individuals already at maximum bandwidth.

Ask any 10 people who work for a company today if they think their job is secure. The majority will tell you "No."

This *you're lucky to have a job* dynamic causes great stress that spills into their work product and their personal life.

Let me give you another example. Let's say you work for a large company in a high stress position. You dodged a bullet and were not included in recent layoffs. But now you're doing the work of two people fighting very tight deadlines. Yes, you're happy you have a job, but you're overwhelmed, overworked, have little or no time to spend with your family and friends and no time for yourself.

Am I hitting a nerve with some of you?

I can relate to the above situation because I've been there. Fear and burnout are becoming more and more common. In my case, I needed to find techniques to keep my sanity while working over 80 hours a week. Let me share with you 2 statements that will help with any stress you may feel when hearing news about changes within your company:

Change is the only constant in life.

You only have control over your reaction!

Having these 2 *beliefs* in your arsenal will allow you to conquer any situation, in and outside of work.

DECREASING CONSIDERATION AND EMPATHY

I've witnessed many executives disrespecting their workforce, some perhaps out of ignorance, but others making statements that demonstrated lack of empathy, compassion and common decency.

Over the years, I've risen in the ranks and have been privy to many levels of management behaving badly. I can write an entire chapter on managers who have demonstrated bad behavior toward their staff, like screaming or berating them, acting with condescendence or being outright mean.

I've been in meetings with senior vice presidents and executives at large corporations where I sat there mouth ajar as they spoke about their workforce as if they were cattle.

One in particular that stays in the forefront of my memory was a tight deadline that fell at the end of December. There were concerns about the sheer number of hours that needed to be worked. One executive even laughed at this mid-December meeting as the final decision was to rescind all planned vacations for staff, only allowing folks to have the single Christmas day holiday off.

I understand deadlines, but thought how this decision lacked consideration, affecting those who already had made plans to spend cherished time with their families during the holiday season.

One of my earliest pet peeves about managers having lack of consideration is being asked to create something for management, only to have it not be utilized. It bothered me when these deliverables were tied to a deadline that caused me to have to work extra hours to achieve them. One of my more memorable experiences with this was when I was working for Linda in New York, who continually provided me with assignments that had me working late into the evening to complete, most of which she never used. When I finally confronted her, asking if there was something incorrect about what I had provided, she replied that she thought they were great, but changed her mind about what she wanted. This does happen in corporate America, but the sheer number attributable to this woman's change in direction was unprecedented.

Another area where I have experienced a manager's lack of consideration was being asked to travel to an outside office without any real need for being there. I will never understand Rosie, who had me travel to Kansas City 3 days a week, to watch the back of her head while we participated in teleconference calls, when I could have easily taken these calls from my home state.

The last example was one of my first experiences, back in the late 1990's. I will never forget that gruesome month when I was personally asked to find a solution to fix a program glitch effecting over 50,000 retirement plan distribution tax statements before the government mandated 1099-R mailing date. It was a very long month as I worked tirelessly performing my regular duties and working late into the evening to solve this issue. I utilized my skills in actuarial science and mathematics, as I came up with the dozen or so 50 step algorithmic formulas to match each incorrect scenario.

It was a Wednesday at the end of January, and I had worked close to 300 hours within a 30 day period, solving the problem and making the mailing deadline, ultimately saving the company over 1 million in penalties.

I was both mentally and physically drained, but being that this was January, I had no accrued sick or vacation time yet for the year. I asked my then manager, Wilhelm, if it would be okay to take off Thursday and Friday. Instead of being thanked for the work I performed and allowing me a little time off to recuperate, he grimaced as he declined my request, waved his hand and stated, "You're lucky you have a job!"

Needless to say, I did not get the break that I needed from my compassionless manager.

UNREASONABLE TIMELINES

Have you ever been given a project deadline that seems so ridiculous that you can't imagine what upper management was thinking?

When I make this statement, I'm not only speaking to the person who ultimately has to perform the work, but all the layers of management between. Every single one of those individuals feels the pressure from the level above them.

Anyone who works in technology certainly knows that timelines are getting shorter and the hours per day to meet these designated due dates are getting longer. You join the day's first meeting before the sun rises and juggle deliverables with turnaround times that twist your head around, not to mention make your heart palpitate as your body overcompensates for the pace.

How do you handle these deadlines and still keep your head above water?

There was a time that a due date, whittled down to an unmanageable point, used to have me jumping out of my skin, feeling anxious, my stomach turning as bile made its way to the back of my throat. Now, however, I take a deep breath and just shake my head, and use several coping mechanisms to better handle the pace.

As we learn to handle the pressures of the corporate world, the best thing we can do is to stay focused. To do this is to learn more about how to compartmentalize our tasks as well as our emotions.

We're trained to organize tasks to help put things into perspective, but our emotions, well, that requires a little different type of work. It is however obtainable.

When management has lost sight of what is truly important in life, show them compassion and don't allow them to ruffle your feathers. Smile knowing that you are not succumbing to the pressure.

My advice to managers who let the stress of their responsibilities get to them, do not subsequently beat down others, but take a moment and allow your workforce the space and a time to do their job.

THE BAIT AND SWITCH

Have you ever had a manager approach you with an opportunity that you know will benefit your career, dangling the carrot, just to take it away?

Let me give you an example. Sally has one-on-one meetings with her manager Bob on Friday afternoons. In one of the meetings, Bob briefly mentioned a very visible project requiring a particular expertise that, because of her years of experience in this area, he wanted to give to Sally. He promised to discuss it in more detail with her at their next weekly one-on-one meeting. He asked Sally to take the upcoming week to think about the information she would need to quickly come up to speed.

Sally walked away from the meeting excited. She danced around the rest of the afternoon knowing that her manager thought so highly of her, that he would trust her with this special project, thrilled that this experience would help further her career.

She spent the next week creating a *To Do* list about what she needed to get up to speed, in preparation for their next meeting. When she met with Bob the following week, she brought up the *To Do* list Bob asked her to think about. He redirected the conversation to other assignments that would be on Sally's plate, none of which were that special assignment they had previously discussed.

Later that day in a general staff meeting, Bob announced that Frank, a less experienced associate, had been awarded the special project. Sally calmly stood there, trying not to show her disappointment. At the end of the meeting she went back to her office, closed the door and sat there stunned for about an hour, before regaining her composure. Sally's initial reaction of remaining calm was wise.

Has this ever happened to you? How would you react?

By taking the higher road you put aside insecurity, envy and jealousy. No one would blame Sally for being bitter. She could have spent time second guessing her abilities. She could have taken a step back and watched to see if Frank failed, but that would not have served her.

So how did Sally ultimately react?

After she composed herself, she found Frank and congratulated him, offering the list that she created. She told him to reach out if he needed any additional help. Frank smiled and thanked her, admitting that he was feeling overwhelmed.

If you've been working for decades like I have, the chances of this situation happening is not uncommon.

All levels of management have a responsibility of providing guidance and opportunities to their direct reports. We'll never know why Bob handed this assignment to the less experienced Frank over the more experienced Sally, but there are a couple of things Bob could have handled better. For example, approaching

Sally and offering her the assignment, then turning around and giving it to someone else was his first mistake. The second was not contacting Sally when the assignment was handed to Frank, having her discover it at a general staff meeting. By doing so, Bob risked losing the respect of one of his senior staff members and worse, took the risk of squashing her enthusiasm, souring her attitude and possibly losing her.

A personal experience with the bait and switch occurred on one of my consulting assignments. I was interviewed by a manager who went by the nickname Chip, with whom I knew I could work well with. This assignment had me relocating across the country. On my first day, Chip sat me down and nonchalantly explained that a reorganization had taken place. He was moving on, I would be reporting to another manager, I was given a project that was a misalignment with my skillset and the project was in flux.

I sat there for a moment, a thousand thoughts racing through my mind. Here I was on my first day, in a new city, spending my savings to move across the country and having signed a year lease in a nearby apartment. I was uncomfortable about the situation that was now thrust upon me.

Although I appreciated his honesty, since the reorganization occurred prior to my start date, it would have been nice to have been provided with this information before I packed up my belongings in storage, gave up my current place of residence and travelled the 3.5 day journey to a new home and job.

What I learned from this experience is that change is inevitable, and our reaction to change is the *only* thing in our control.

I could have reacted, but chose not to. I turned to him shrugging my shoulders stating, "Welcome to corporate America."

Only time would tell if I'd be laid off. In the meantime, I was going to do what I came here for. It would be months before any final decisions would be made and I was going to make the best of it, not allowing this limbo period get to me.

DECISION STALLING

I remember a project where I needed resources with specific skills. As soon as it became evident, I put in my request. I was not the resource manager, so had to rely on external sources for the funding approval. May came and went, as well as June.

Every week I checked on the status, knowing that the project would not be able to move forward without the talent to perform critical tasks. The answer was continually the same: "We will be meeting about this in the coming weeks."

I followed the project manager handbook and entered these risks into the project status. It was not until I finally turned the project yellow, that upper management took notice.

Alas, they were still not ready to make any decisions regarding funding. In the end, the project had to be put on hold until such time that funding for the resources requested could be filled.

I love to throw the word 'frustration' out there. In cases like this, that is the best word to describe that feeling of helplessness that ensues when you know what you need, but am unable to obtain it. My personal learning from these experiences is to remember that we should not hold on to anything that is out of our control.

MANAGER RISING

I used to get frustrated when I'd see someone who was not as good as I was get promoted over me, especially when we were out for the same position. The news would have me meandering down to the local bar, sobbing in my Jack and coke for several evenings in a row as I tried to figure out why. I worked more hours, produced more quality work, nonetheless they were somehow viewed as better that I was.

What is it that has those less intelligent people rising up the latter when poor hard-working schmucks like me were stuck on lower rungs?

Someone very wise described it to me so it finally made sense, making me see it from a more holistic perspective.

If you're successfully doing the work of two, management is not willing to lose that resource by promoting them to a management position. Not at first, anyway.

I know this sounds contradictory to the premise of work hard and get rewarded, but it's true.

What should you do when you experience the rise of other less qualified people at the workplace?
There's only one thing you can do without driving yourself to envy, jealousy and resentment. Be happy for them.

Management is always looking for the stars that have the entire combination, those that have found the balance between work and home and who have learned how to juggle, switch gears and adapt.

This is your opportunity to shine brighter by seeing not their shortcomings, but what they did right and try and emulate it.

My hope is that after reading these words you come away with some insight, tips and a different perception of the people that you spend most of your waking hours with.

Know that your reaction is the key to the control you have over your world.

LD Forester

The End